Georgia's
Goods and Services

Christina Hill, M.A.

Consultants

Regina Holland, Ed.S., *Henry County Schools*
Christina Noblet, Ed.S., *Paulding County
    School District*
Jennifer Troyer, *Paulding County Schools*

Publishing Credits

Rachelle Cracchiolo, M.S.Ed., *Publisher*
Conni Medina, M.A.Ed., *Managing Editor*
Emily R. Smith, M.A.Ed., *Series Developer*
Diana Kenney, M.A.Ed., NBCT, *Content Director*
Torrey Maloof, *Editor*
Courtney Patterson, *Multimedia Designer*

Image Credits: pp.2,15,32 LOC [LC-DIG-pga-04657]; p.5
John Lund/Marc Romanelli/Blend Images/Corbis; p.6
WendellandCarolyn/Getty Images; p.8 Jason Hawkes/
CORBIS; p.10 Joanna Cepuchowicz / EyeEm/Getty
Images; p.11 LOC [LC-USF34- 043994-D]; p.13 Mikki
Ansin/Getty Images; pp.18,31 PHOTO MEDIA/Corbis; p.20
John Sommers II/Reuters/Corbis, Justin Sullivan/Getty
Images; p.23 Bloomberg/Getty Images, Mav/Wikimedia
Commons; pp.2,5,13 LC [LC-USZ62-66417001]; All other
images iStock and/or Shutterstock.

Teacher Created Materials

5301 Oceanus Drive
Huntington Beach, CA 92649-1030
http://www.tcmpub.com

ISBN 978-1-4938-2563-9

© 2017 Teacher Created Materials, Inc.

Table of Contents

Our Economy

Have you ever traded toys with your best friend? This is called the **barter** system. Long ago, people had to barter to get things. This means they had to trade. But it was hard to find the things they needed. So people started using money to buy things. This made it much easier for them to buy and sell things.

In Georgia, there is a system of buying and selling things. Bills and coins are used. This is called an **economy** (ih-KAHN-uh-mee). People work hard to earn money. They can use that money to buy the things they need.

Top Ten!

In 2015, Georgia had the tenth largest economy in the United States.

Then

A Georgia dentist uses the barter system.

Now

A teen pays for his purchase at a store.

Care to Trade?

People could only trade or buy things from people who lived nearby long ago. Today, things are much different. People can ship things on a boat. Or they can ship things on an airplane. They can buy things that are made all over the world!

Some countries sell things that are not made in the United States. These are called **imports**. The United States also sells things to other countries. These are called **exports**. Georgia has good weather for growing crops. It exports food such as peanuts and peaches.

Millions of Peaches

Georgia sells 86 million pounds of peaches each year. Peaches grow well in the mild winters and hot summers.

This oil refinery turns oil into products people can use.

Key Resources

Things that are made to be sold come from **resources**. Natural resources are things like water, wood, oil, and plants. They are found in nature. These things are used to build homes. They are also used to drive cars and make clothes.

Some resources are limited. That means that there is only a certain amount. More cannot be made. Oil is a limited resource. It takes millions of years for it to be made under the ground. That is why these resources need to be **conserved**, not wasted.

The Okefenokee Wildlife Refuge is a place where plants and animals are protected.

Georgia companies bring money into the state. They do this by selling items that are made from resources found there. There are forests full of pine trees in the state. Over 60 percent of the state is covered in trees!

These trees are sold for lots of things. The wood is used to build homes. It can also be made into paper. But a tree is gone forever once it is cut down. Another tree needs to be planted in its place. This way, the state will not run out of wood to sell.

Men cut lumber in 1941 with the help of mules.

Paper Products

Georgia-Pacific makes many paper products. It sells paper towels, toilet paper, and paper cups.

Plentiful Goods

Goods are things that can be bought and sold. Food and games are goods. So are cars and homes. **Consumers** are the people who buy these goods.

Producers make the goods that are for sale. Many goods are made in Georgia. In fact, the state is the number one producer of peanuts and pecans in the nation! That means it sells more of these goods than any other state.

Mr. President

President Jimmy Carter was a producer and a president. He grew and sold peanuts.

This is President Jimmy Carter's peanut farm today.

Dr. John Pemberton

Dr. John Pemberton made a soft drink in 1886. Now, it is one of Georgia's most famous goods. He thought it tasted great. He started the Coca-Cola **Company** to sell his new product.

John sold his product at a store for 5 cents per glass. He sold 9 colas per day in the first year. This product is now sold in 200 countries. There are 1.9 billion Coca-Colas® sold each day around the world. Now that's a lot of cola!

Canned Cola

Coca-Cola® was not sold in cans until 1960. That's 74 years after the drink was first made!

1890 Coca-Cola advertisement

The Home Depot is a big company in Georgia. It sells goods for fixing things. It also sells goods for making things. Homes may need new paint or floors. This store sells the tools people need to fix their homes on their own. Many people think that fixing things on their own saves money.

The Home Depot's owners started with two stores in Atlanta in 1978. Many people shopped there. So they built more stores. Today, they have thousands of stores in the country.

DIY

DIY stands for "do-it-yourself." DIY projects might include building a tree house, a birdhouse, or a garden.

At Your Service

Do not forget that goods are things that you can buy. These are items that you can use or touch. But a service is different. A service is work or help that is for sale. People get paid to do services.

There are many kinds of services. Teaching students is a service. Giving a haircut is a service. Fixing a car or raking leaves in a yard are also services. Have you ever sold a service?

A boy delivers newspapers on his bike in 1966.

Walking dogs for other people is a service.

N146UP

UPS?

UPS stands for "United Parcel Service." A parcel is a box or large envelope that is sent to a person.

UPS is a big company. Its main office is in Georgia. It sells services. It helps people ship things. This means that they help people move goods to other places. Maybe you have seen their big brown trucks in your town.

UPS started shipping things in 1907. Workers had to walk or ride bikes to deliver goods. Today, UPS ships to more than 200 countries. Workers ship goods on airplanes and ships. The goods often arrive quickly.

Low Emission
Hybrid Electric Vehicle

Worldwide
Synchronizing the

Have you ever been to an airport? Have you ever flown on an airplane? If so, you have probably heard of Delta Air Lines. It is based in Atlanta. It sells a service. It helps people travel.

Their first airplanes were crop dusters. They dropped a kind of dust over plants to kill bugs. Then, their pilots started flying bigger airplanes that carried people. Many people like to fly on airplanes. It is a fast way to travel. People fly all over the world on Delta's airplanes.

AIR LINES

Flying High

Delta's home base is Hartsfield-Jackson airport in Atlanta. It is one of the busiest airports in the world!

Need or Want?

The way people buy goods and services has changed over time. Today, money is used instead of bartering. People shop at stores in their town. They buy things on the Internet.

But one thing has not changed: goods and services are either needs or wants. Food and water are needs. So are homes and clothes. People need these things to survive. But toys, games, or movie tickets are wants. It is important to make sure you have money for your needs first. Then, you can make choices about buying the things you want.

People can buy goods on the Internet.

Your Role

Georgia is a state full of resources. There are many goods and services for sale. That means the state has a strong economy.

You are probably already a consumer. But are you a producer? Are there services you can do to earn money? Think about what you want to do when you grow up. Will you sell a good? Will you farm land and sell crops? Will you be a pilot or a doctor? Whatever you choose, you will play a role in the state's economy.

Chart It!

We buy goods and services every day. Make a chart to list all the things your family buys or pays for this week. Then, mark whether each item is a good or a service. Did you pay any bills? Did you go somewhere fun? Did you eat in a restaurant or shop for food at a market?

Review the chart with your family. Talk about which things are needs and which are wants.

Money Spent	Good	Service
school lunch	X	
movie theater ticket		X
car wash		X
pencils	X	
new jacket	X	
gas for car	X	
dog groomer		X

Glossary

barter—to trade things for other things instead of for money

company—a business that makes, buys, or sells a good or service for money

conserved—used something carefully to prevent loss or waste

consumers—people who buy goods and services

economy—the system of buying and selling goods and services

exports—goods sent to another country to be sold

imports—goods brought into a country to be sold

producers—people who make goods and provide services

resources—things a country has that can be used to make things

Index

Your Turn!

All Dressed Up

This is an advertisement for Coca-Cola. The artist
drew a woman in fancy clothing. Why do you think
the artist drew her that way? Create an advertisement
for a good or service. What will you draw? What will
you write?